MW00813039

The Test Tutor's

Practice Test
for the
Kaufman Brief Intelligence Test™ 2

KBIT™-2

(Ages 4 —12)

Test Tutor Publishing, LLC

Kaufman Brief Intelligence Test™ II - (KBIT™-II) is a registered trademark of NCS Pearson, Inc. NCS Pearson, Inc. is not affiliated with, nor does it endorse or sponsor the contents of this book.

The Test Tutor

Practice Test
for the

Kaufman Brief Intelligence Test™ 2 (KBIT™2)

(Ages 4 —12)

© 2013 Test Tutor Publishing, LLC

Printed in the United States of America
November 2013

All rights reserved. No part of this book may be reproduced in any form whatsoever, by photography, electronically or by any other means, without permission in writing from the publisher.

Test Tutor Publishing, LLC presents all material without warranty of any kind, express or implied. Test Tutor Publishing is not liable for the accuracy of any description, or for mistakes, errors or omissions of any kind, and is not responsible for any loss or damage caused by a user's reliance on the information contained in Test Tutor publications or website. All of the information contained herein is subject to change without notice, and users are advised to confirm all information about a product or service before making any commitments.

Kaufman Brief Intelligence Test™ II - (KBIT™-II) is a registered trademark of NCS Pearson, Inc. NCS Pearson, Inc. is not affiliated with, nor does it endorse or sponsor the contents of this book.

TABLE OF CONTENTS

About Test Tutor Publishing

Our philosophy is that any child can achieve exceptional test results and academic success, with practice. Our products help children of all abilities improve their performance on standardized tests, by focusing on building critical thinking skills, employing test-taking strategies, and reducing test anxiety.

At Test Tutor Publishing, our mission is to create content-rich, reasonably-priced, user-friendly test preparation materials that empower children to achieve at their highest level. All of our products have been created by experienced educators and psychologists and are based on the latest educational research. Since 2010, we have helped thousands of students prepare for school-related tests with our colorful, fun and easy-to-use workbooks and interactive games.

The Kaufman Brief Intelligence Test™ Explained

The Kaufman Brief Intelligence Test™, Second Edition (KBIT™-2) measures verbal and non-verbal intelligence in individuals from ages 4 through 90 years. It is administered to individuals, not groups, by a counseling or psychological professional, and usually takes 15 to 30 minutes to complete.

The KBIT™-2 test is comprised of three subtests: verbal knowledge, riddles, and matrices and yields three scores: verbal, nonverbal and overall (known as the IQ composite). The verbal score, based on the results of the verbal knowledge and riddles subtests, measures word knowledge, general information retention, and ability to form verbal concepts and reason. The nonverbal score, based on the matrices subtest, assesses a person's ability to make visual analogies and recognize spatial relationships.

How the KBIT™-2 Test is Scored

The raw score, which is the total number of correct answers, is converted to a standard score. Average standard scores range from 85 to 115. Standard scores that are 131 and greater are described as "upper extreme."

How to Use this Practice Test

This practice test is designed to give your child practice and familiarity with the skills and concepts necessary for success on the KBIT™-2 test. It consists of 160 practice items divided into three subtests with corresponding answer keys. It was developed to identify your child's testing strengths and weaknesses so that you can thoroughly prepare your child for the test. It is not designed to give a test score or percentile rank because it has not been standardized with the KBIT®-2 norms and standards.

Before you begin test preparation, thoroughly read through the practice test. When you are ready to begin testing, seat your child at a table and chair in a quiet, well-lit room. Tell your child that you are going to play a series of games with him and that he can take breaks as needed. Review the testing instructions with your child. During the practice administration, circle or write your child's responses on the answer sheet. If your child answers four questions in a row incorrectly, he/she may need a brief rest or may need to move on to a new activity. If so, feel free to proceed to a new subtest and finish the previous subtest at a later time.

Additionally, for optimal results when administering the test, praise your child's efforts and encourage your child to do his best independently. Once the practice exercises are completed, check your child's answers with the answer key. Then, use the responses to evaluate your child's strengths and weaknesses.

Description
Your child will be asked to identify pictures that illustrate a word or answer a question.

Instructions
Begin this subtest at the question appropriate for the child's age:

Age 4-5 begin with question 1
Age 6-7 begin with question 3
Age 8 begin with question 9
Age 9-10 begin with question 15
Age 11-12 begin with question 18

Follow the instructions at the top of each page. Circle your child's responses in the practice test. The correct responses can be found beginning on page 100. Begin with item #1 by saying: **"Point to the watch."**

1

A	B	C
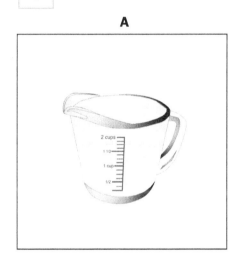	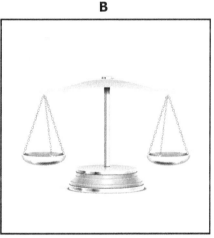	

D	E	F

2

Instructions
SAY: "Point to the coin."

A

B

C

D

E

F

3

<u>Instructions</u>
SAY: "Point to utensils."

A

B

C

D

E

F

4

Instructions
SAY: "Point to hug."

A

B

C

D

E

F

5

Instructions
SAY: "Point to giving."

A

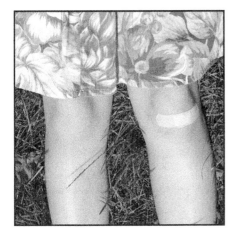

B

C

D

E

F

6

Instructions
SAY: "Point to rain."

A **B** **C**

D **E** **F**

7

Instructions
SAY: "Point to the rat."

A

B

C

D

E

F

8

<u>Instructions</u>
SAY: "Point to light."

A

B

C

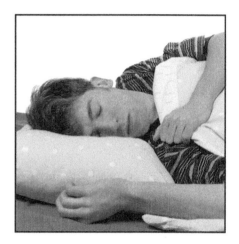

D

E

F

9

<u>Instructions</u>
SAY: "Point to what goes with Spring."

A   B   C

D   E   F

10

SAY: "Point to conversing."

A

B

C

D

E

F

11

<u>Instructions</u>
SAY: "Point to what lives in the jungle."

A

B

C

D

E

F

12

Instructions
SAY: "Point to a mob."

A

B

C

D

E

F

13

Instructions
SAY: "Point to gulp."

A

B

C

D

E

F

14

Instructions
SAY: "Point to the amphibian."

A

B

C

D

E

F

Verbal Knowledge

15

Instructions
SAY: "Point to slippery."

A

B

C

D

E

F

16

Instructions
SAY: "Point to exit."

A

B

C

D

E

F

17

Instructions
SAY: "Point to something that tells you how long something is."

A

B

C

D

E

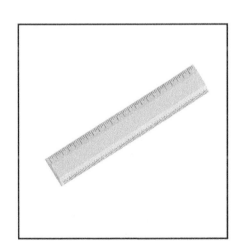

F

18

SAY: "Point to abrasion."

A

B

C

D

E

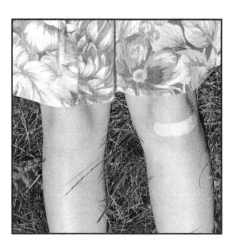

F

19

Instructions
SAY: "Point to sliding."

A

B

C

D

E

F

20

<u>Instructions</u>
SAY: "Point to laborer."

A

B

C

D

E

F

21

Instructions
SAY: "Point to what you use to think."

A

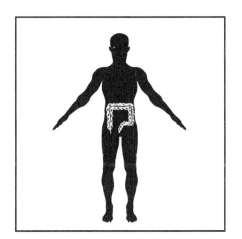

B

C

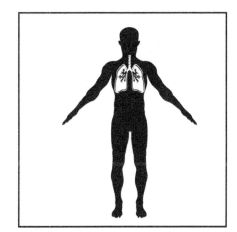

D

E

F

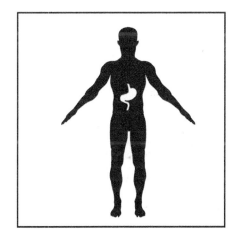

22

SAY: "Point to athlete."

A

B

C

D

E

F

23

Instructions
SAY: "Point to banister."

A

B

C

D

E

F

24

Instructions
SAY: "Point to feline."

A

B

C

D

E

F

25

Instructions
SAY: "Point to ancient."

A

B

C

D

E

F

26

Instructions
SAY: "Point to sanitize."

A

B

C

D

E

F

27

Instructions
SAY: "Point to opulence."

A

B

C

D

E

F

28

Instructions
SAY: "Point to clench."

A

B

C

D

E

F

29

Instructions
SAY: "Point to triumphant."

A

B

C

D

E

F

30

Instructions
SAY: "Point to incandescent."

A

B

C

D

E

F

31

Instructions
SAY: "Point to the home of the President of the United States."

A

B

C

D

E

F

32

Instructions
SAY: "Point to condensation."

A

B

C

D

E

F

33

Instructions
SAY: "Point to educational."

A

B

C

D

E

F

34

SAY: "Point to recovery."

A

B

C

D

E

F

35

Instructions
SAY: "Point to exploration."

A

B

C

D

E

F

36

Instructions
SAY: "Point to the insignia."

A

B

C

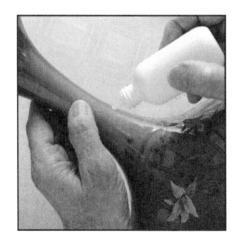

D

E

F

37

Instructions
SAY: "Point to procuring."

A

B

C

D

E

F

38

SAY: "Point to pacify."

A

B

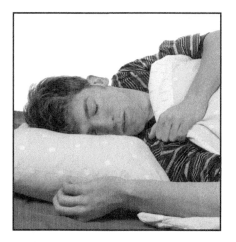

C

D

E

F

39

Instructions
SAY: "Point to the chanteuse."

A   B   C

D   E   F

40

Instructions
SAY: "Point to contention."

A

B

C

D

E

F

41

Instructions
SAY: "Point to the location of the cardiac organ."

A

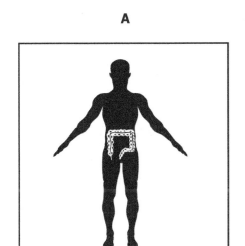

B

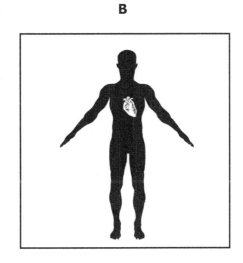

C

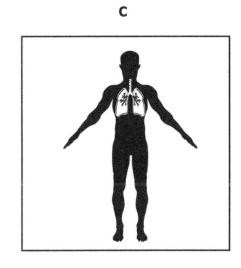

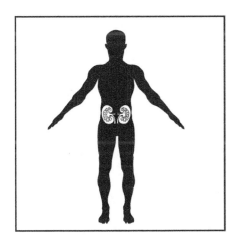

D

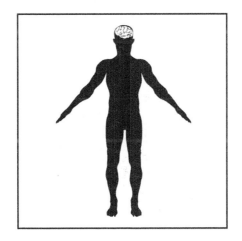

E

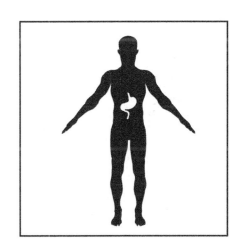

F

42

Instructions
SAY: "Point to introvert."

A

B

C

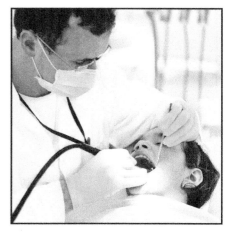

D

E

F

43

Instructions
SAY: "Point to impede."

A

B

C

D

E

F

44

SAY: "Point to the procession."

A

B

C

D

E

F

45

Instructions
SAY: "Point to pollution."

A

B

C

D

E

F

46

<u>Instructions</u>
SAY: "Point to ignite."

A

B

C

D

E

F

47

Instructions
SAY: "Point to toil."

A

B

C

D

E

F

48

Instructions
SAY: "Point to frivolity."

A

B

C

D

E

F

49

Instructions
SAY: "Point to haggard."

A

B

C

D

E

F

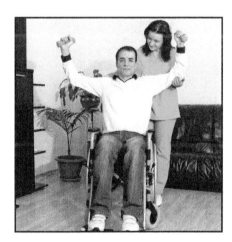

50

Instructions
SAY: "Point to malleable."

A

B

C

D

E

F

Description

Your child must choose the correct response to complete a matrix. The items represent both real items and abstract designs.

Instructions

Begin this subtest at the question appropriate for your child's age:

Age 4-7 begin with question 1
Age 8-12 begin with question 10

Point to the exercises and say:

> **"Let's play a game. Look at this object** (Point to the single square or matrix) **and tell me which one here** (point to bottom pictures) **goes with this one here?"** Point to the single square or the square with the question mark.

Your child must either point to the answer or say the number of the answer. Circle your child's responses in the practice test. After the subtest is completed, review the correct responses beginning on page 102. Explain to your child why the correct answer completes the matrix.

1

| 1 | 2 | 3 | 4 | 5 |

2

1	2	3	4	5

3

1	2	3	4	5

4

1	2	3	4	5

5

1	2	3	4	5

6

1	2	3	4	5

7

1	2	3	4	5

8

1	2	3	4	5

9

1	2	3	4	5

10

1	2	3	4	5	6

11

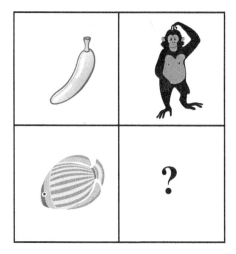

1	2	3	4	5	6

12

1	2	3	4	5	6

13

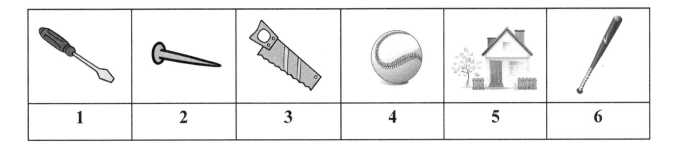

1	2	3	4	5	6

14

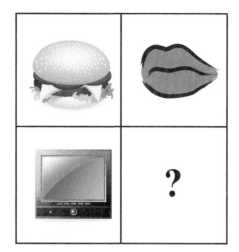

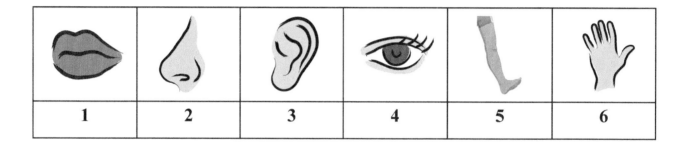

| 1 | 2 | 3 | 4 | 5 | 6 |

15

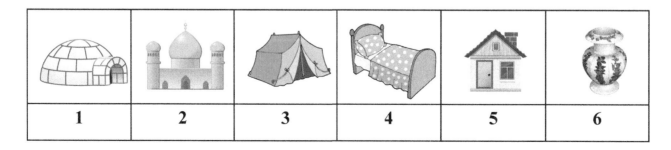

| 1 | 2 | 3 | 4 | 5 | 6 |

16

1	2	3	4	5	6

17

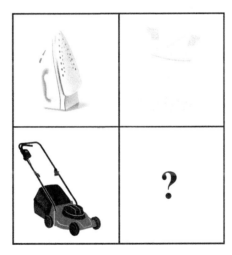

1	2	3	4	5	6

18

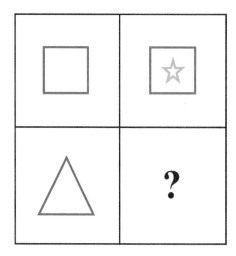

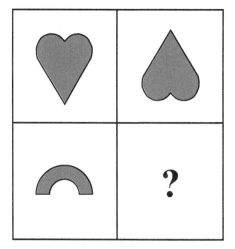

1	2	3	4	5	6

19

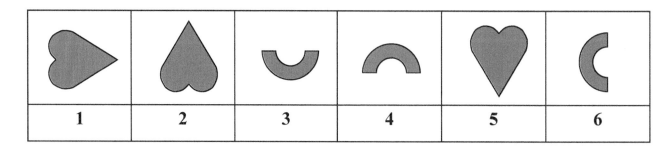

1	2	3	4	5	6

20

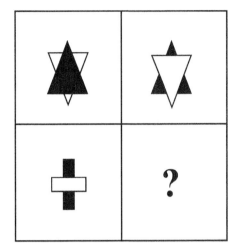

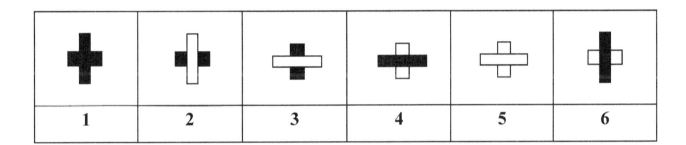

1	2	3	4	5	6

21

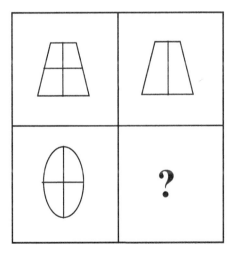

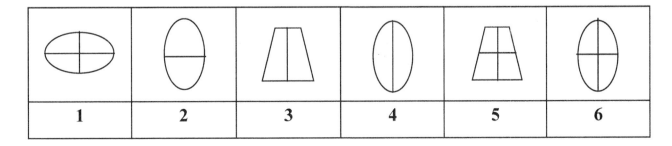

1	2	3	4	5	6

22

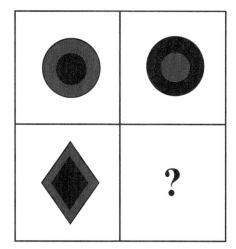

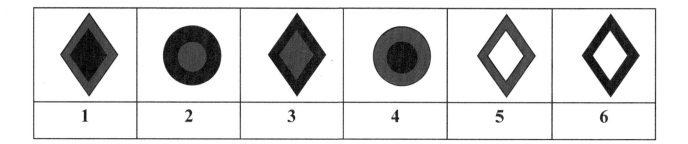

23

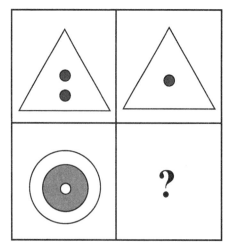

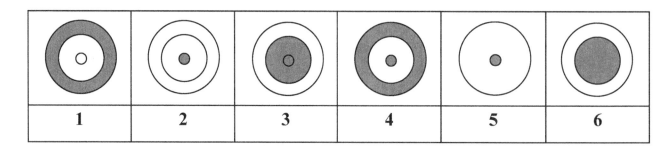

24

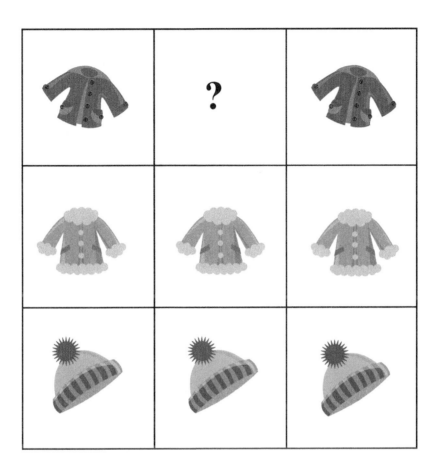

| 1 | 2 | 3 | 4 | 5 | 6 |

25

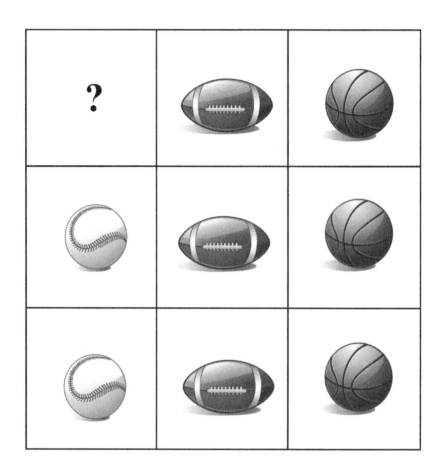

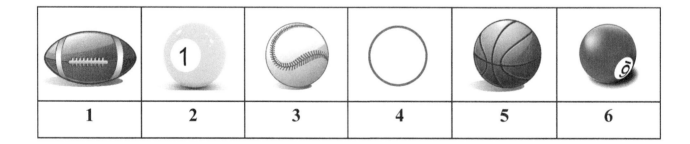

26

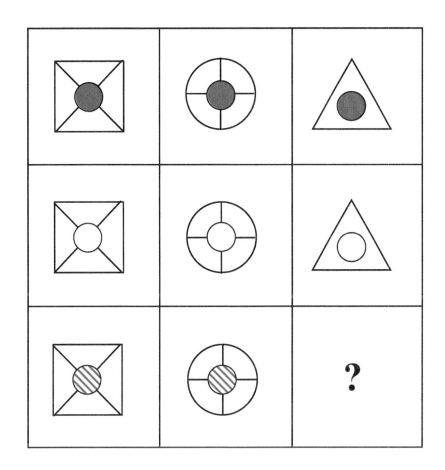

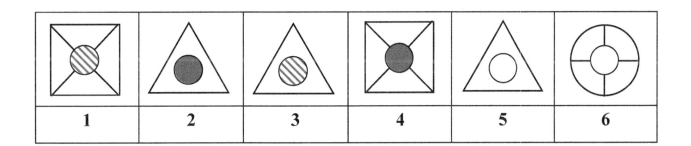

27

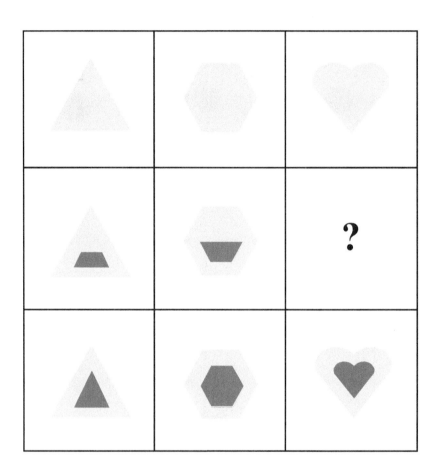

| 1 | 2 | 3 | 4 | 5 | 6 |

28

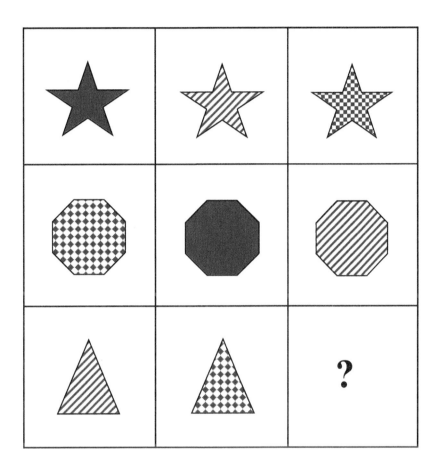

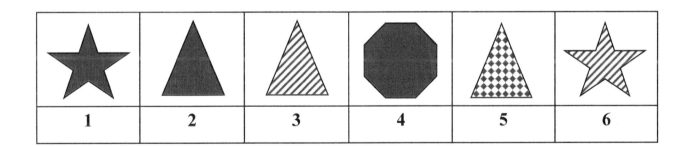

| 1 | 2 | 3 | 4 | 5 | 6 |

29

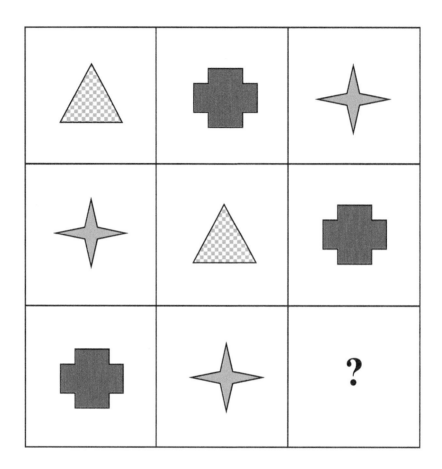

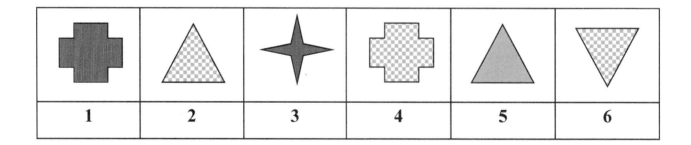

| 1 | 2 | 3 | 4 | 5 | 6 |

30

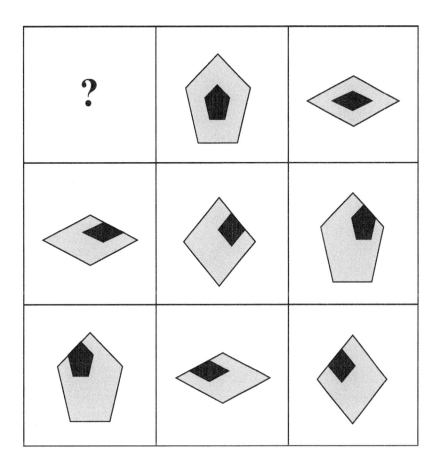

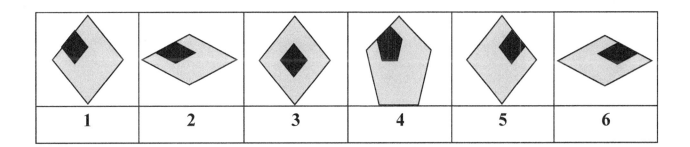

| 1 | 2 | 3 | 4 | 5 | 6 |

31

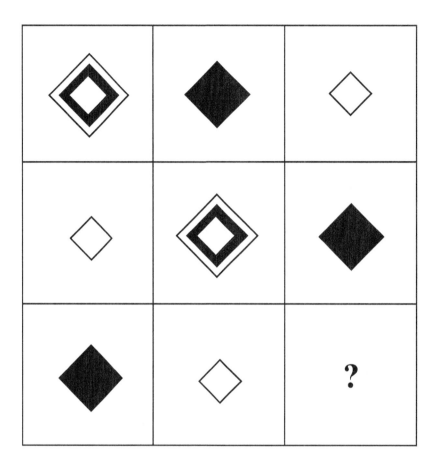

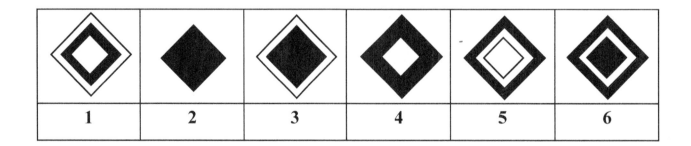

32

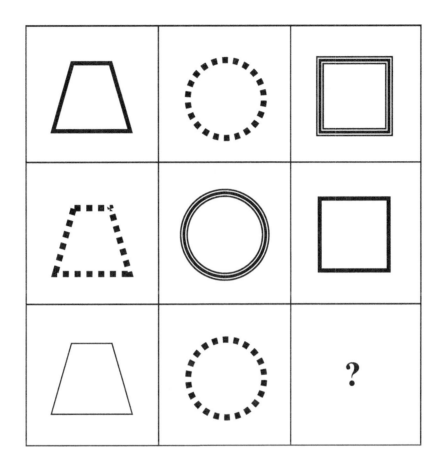

| 1 | 2 | 3 | 4 | 5 | 6 |

33

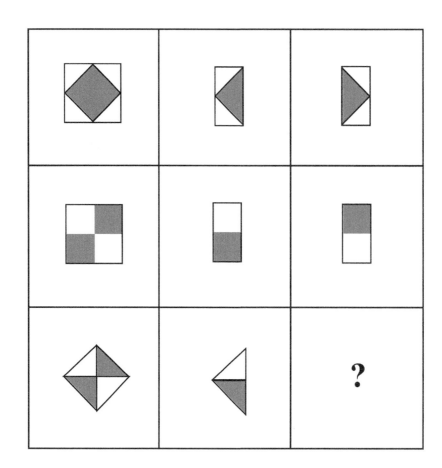

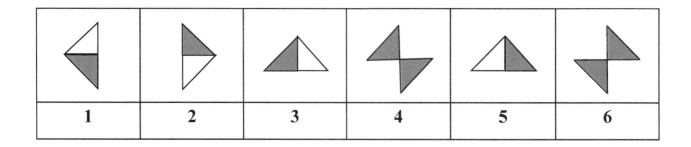

34

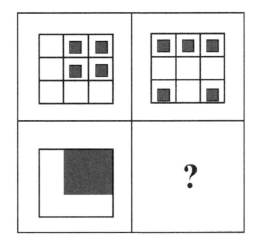

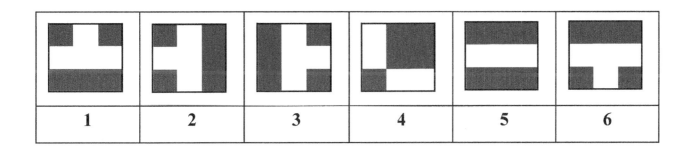

| 1 | 2 | 3 | 4 | 5 | 6 |

35

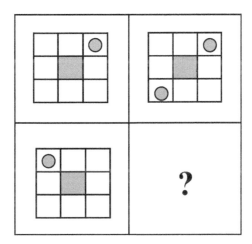

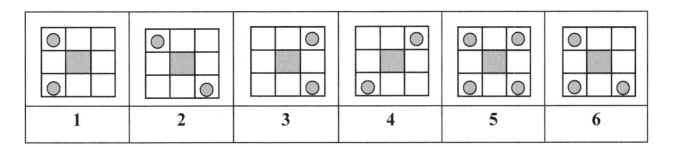

| 1 | 2 | 3 | 4 | 5 | 6 |

36

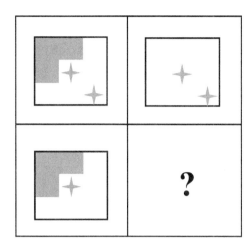

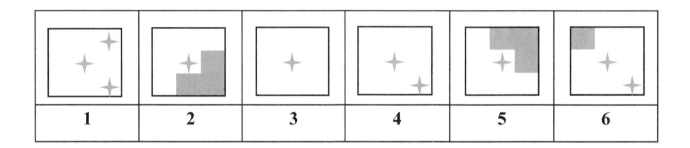

1	2	3	4	5	6

37

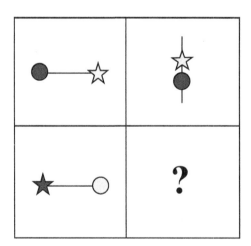

1	2	3	4	5	6

38

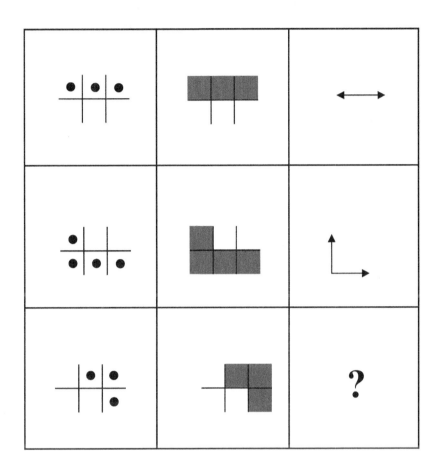

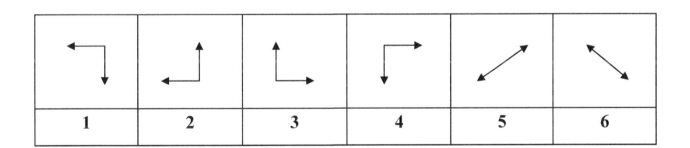

| 1 | 2 | 3 | 4 | 5 | 6 |

39

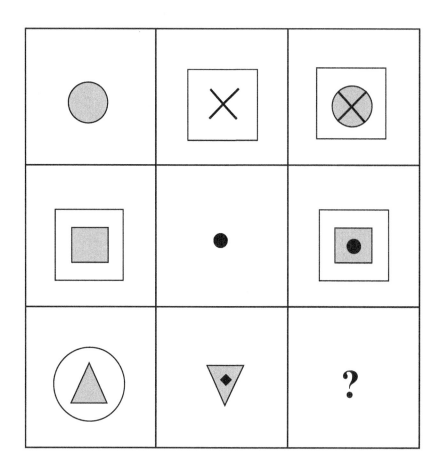

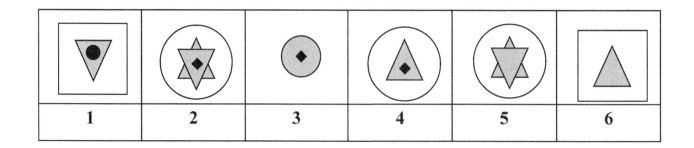

| 1 | 2 | 3 | 4 | 5 | 6 |

40

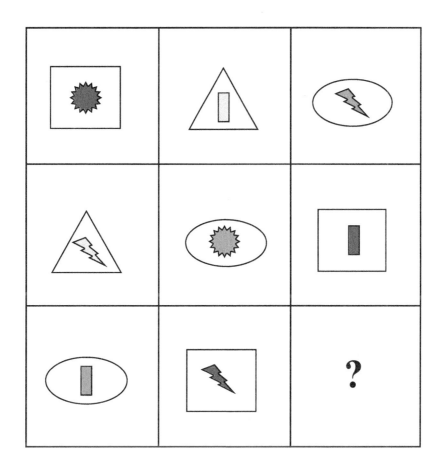

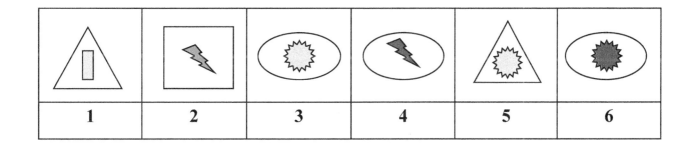

| 1 | 2 | 3 | 4 | 5 | 6 |

41

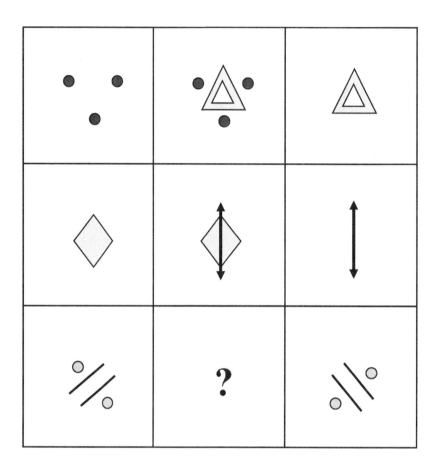

1	2	3	4	5	6

42

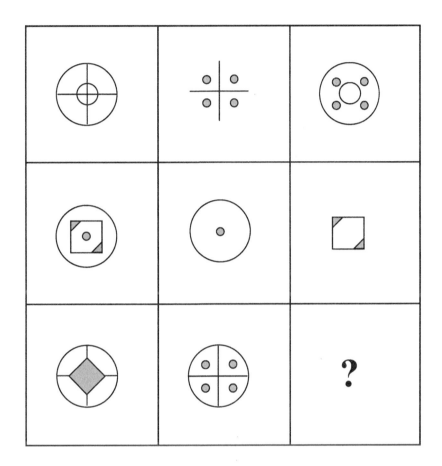

| 1 | 2 | 3 | 4 | 5 | 6 |

43

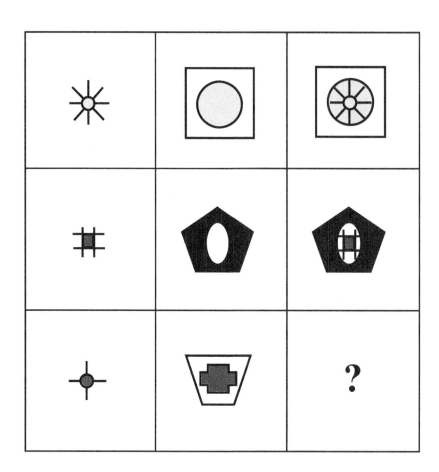

1	2	3	4	5	6

44

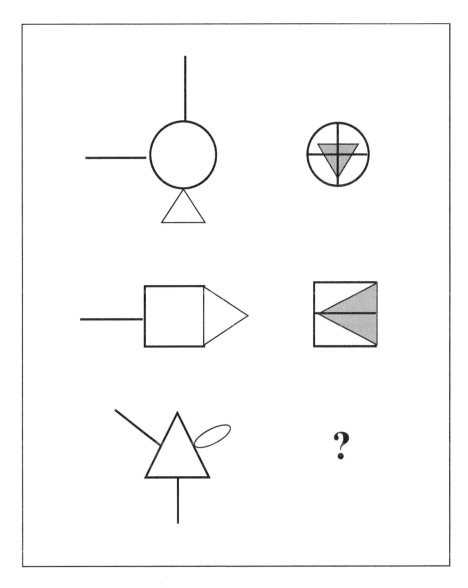

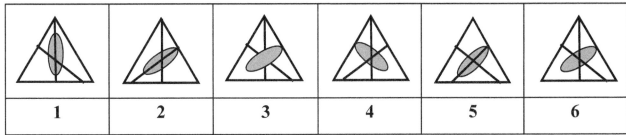

| 1 | 2 | 3 | 4 | 5 | 6 |

45

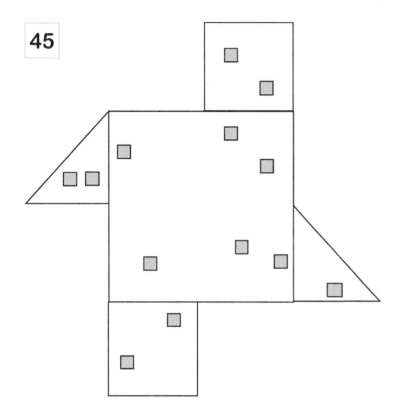

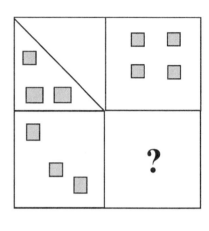

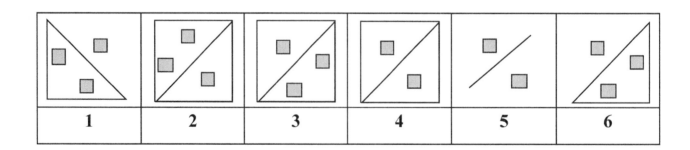

| 1 | 2 | 3 | 4 | 5 | 6 |

46

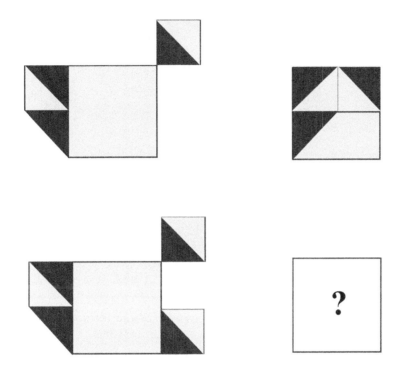

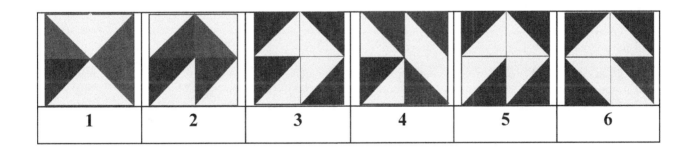

| 1 | 2 | 3 | 4 | 5 | 6 |

47

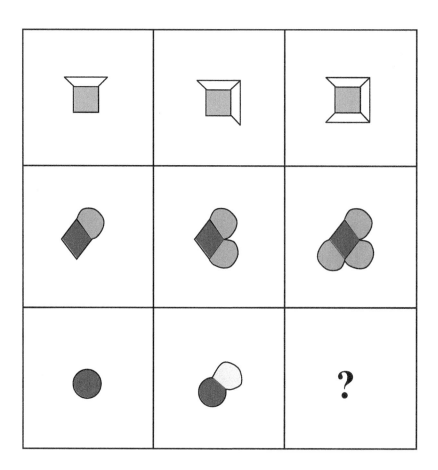

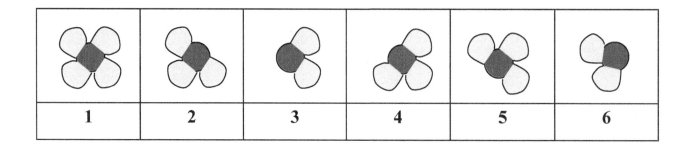

48

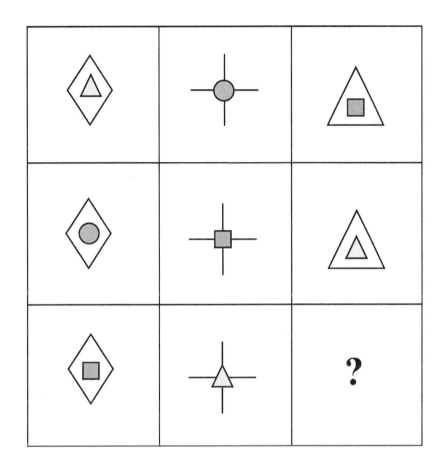

49

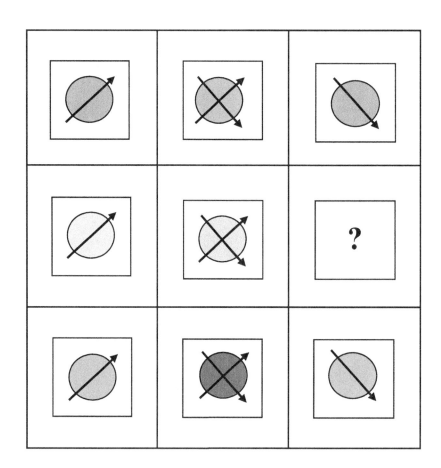

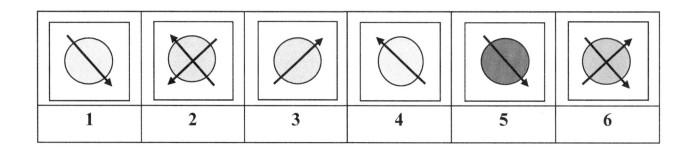

50

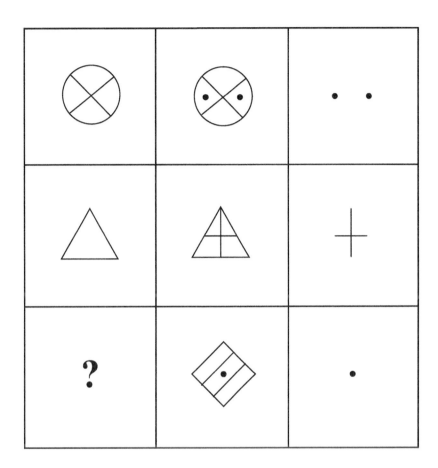

1	2	3	4	5	6

51

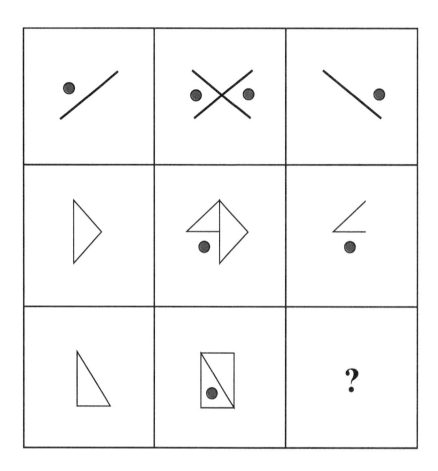

| 1 | 2 | 3 | 4 | 5 | 6 |

Riddles

Description
Your child will be asked to point to a picture or say a word that answers a riddle spoken by the examiner. The test will discontinue after your child gives four consecutive incorrect answers.

Instructions
Begin this subtest at the question appropriate for your child's age:

Age 4-6 begin with question 1
Age 7-11 begin with question 9
Age 12 begin with question 14

Read the clues to your child. Write or circle your child's responses in the practice test.

1. Look at these pictures *(point to the pictures below)*. Point to something that you wear on your head. (hat)

2. Point to something sweet that monkeys eat. (banana)

3. Point to something that you can sit on. (chair)

4. Point to something that you ride in that has wheels. (bus)

5. Now look at the pictures on this page *(point to the pictures below)*. Point to something that chirps and has feathers. (bird)

6. Point to something round that floats. (balloon)

7. Point to something that you have two of that helps you pick things up. (hand)

8. Point to something that is made from milk. (cheese)

SAY: I'm going to ask you a few more questions. Please give me a one-word answer.

Read the clues to your child. Write your child's responses on the scoring form on page 104.

9. What is something that swims and has scales? (fish)

10. What jumps, has a pouch and has a baby called a joey? (kangaroo)

11. What holds a single serving of liquid such as coffee or tea? (cup)

12. What is sweet, is in cakes and can be powdered? (sugar)

13. What is bright, in the sky and makes daytime? (sun)

14. What room has a stove, a refrigerator and a sink? (kitchen)

15. What is something with numbers, hands and a face that people wear on their wrists? (watch)

16. What has rows of food, produce, a meat department and a cashier? (grocery store; supermarket)

17. What tool has teeth and grooms your hair? (comb)

18. What is a folded piece of metal that holds stacks of paper together in the corner? (paper clip; staple)

19. What holds books, and is worn by students and has straps? (backpack; book bag)

20. What is made of rubber, is round and is found on a bicycle? (wheel; tire)

21. What has bristles and is used for oral hygiene? (toothbrush)

22. What has a bulb, emits light and can be found on a side table? (lamp)

23. What is black and white, has keys and has pedals? (piano)

24. What allows sunlight into the home, allows people to see outside and has a screen? (windows)

25. What goes around your neck, is used when eating, and is used to protect clothing (bib)

26. What is worn on the head by bicyclist and keeps your skull safe in a crash? (helmet)

27. What is spoken or written by a person who is grateful for the acts of another person? (thank you)

28. What burns, holds a flame and is made of wood or paper? (match)

29. Who prepares the food and sets the menu at a restaurant? (chef)

30. What is used with water to wash your hands? (soap)

31. What is a box, has a post and holds deliveries? (mailbox)

32. What is a shape and a precious gemstone? (diamond)

33. Where do you deposit your money, have an account and take out loans? (bank)

34. What has bark, leaves, roots and grows? (tree)

35. What frames a window and can be drawn closed to keep light out? (curtains; blinds)

36. What is used to circulate air and has blades? (fan)

37. What has four legs, a flat top and meals can be eaten on it? (table)

38. What can appear suddenly, last for a few minutes or days, and makes the ground wet? (rain, storm)

39. What snack do you eat at a movie that is salty and can be buttered? (popcorn)

40. What is brown, made from a nut, and is often eaten with jelly? (peanut butter)

41. What object is found in oysters and begins as a grain of sand? (pearl)

42. What is made of canvas, can hang between two trees and is great for a nap? (hammock)

43. What sport is played on grass with a clubs and has 18 holes? (golf)

44. What board game has pawns, knights, bishops, kings and queens? (chess)

45. What was once the ninth planet and is now known as a dwarf planet? (Pluto)

46. What officially seals a contract, is known as your autograph and is also known as your John Hancock? (signature)

47. Who asks people questions, writes or speaks about current events and sometimes travels to far away locations? (journalist)

48. What is part of a play, has scenes and is memorized? (script)

49. What is a type of picture that is large and painted on a wall? (mural)

50. Where do you go that has a playground, basketball courts and benches? (park)

51. What are written expressions of affection given on February 14th? (valentines)

52. What is something you can give to someone, has no cost and describes a temperature? (a cold)

53. What Japanese art consists of folding paper to make figures such as animals, shapes or flowers? (origami)

54. What housing is used for camping and to protect you from the elements? (tent)

55. What belongs to a person, is last, and is shared among family members? (surname)

56. What is made of paper, is a punishment, and is given out by police officers? (ticket; fine)

57. What is not reality, used as entertainment and is created by writers? (fiction)

58. What is small, round and indicates that a sentence is complete? (period)

59. What is old, often found underground and is proof of ancient civilizations? (artifact)

Exercise	Child's Response	Correct Answer	Correct?	
1		E	Yes	No
2		B	Yes	No
3		C	Yes	No
4		C	Yes	No
5		F	Yes	No
6		B	Yes	No
7		E	Yes	No
8		A	Yes	No
9		A	Yes	No
10		B	Yes	No
11		A	Yes	No
12		E	Yes	No
13		E	Yes	No
14		B	Yes	No
15		E	Yes	No
16		A	Yes	No
17		E	Yes	No
18		F	Yes	No
19		B	Yes	No
20		B	Yes	No
21		E	Yes	No
22		C	Yes	No
23		B	Yes	No
24		D	Yes	No
25		A	Yes	No

Verbal Knowledge **ANSWER KEY**

Exercise	Child's Response	Correct Answer	Correct?
26		C	Yes No
27		B	Yes No
28		E	Yes No
29		C	Yes No
30		B	Yes No
31		B	Yes No
32		C	Yes No
33		C	Yes No
34		E	Yes No
35		C	Yes No
36		B	Yes No
37		C	Yes No
38		C	Yes No
39		D	Yes No
40		B	Yes No
41		B	Yes No
42		E	Yes No
43		C	Yes No
44		B	Yes No
45		B	Yes No
46		D	Yes No
47		E	Yes No
48		A	Yes No
49		B	Yes No
50		D	Yes No

Total Correct _____

Exercise	Child's Response	Correct Answer	Correct?	
1		5	Yes	No
2		2	Yes	No
3		3	Yes	No
4		2	Yes	No
5		1	Yes	No
6		5	Yes	No
7		4	Yes	No
8		2	Yes	No
9		1	Yes	No
10		5	Yes	No
11		3	Yes	No
12		5	Yes	No
13		2	Yes	No
14		4	Yes	No
15		5	Yes	No
16		2	Yes	No
17		2	Yes	No
18		1	Yes	No
19		3	Yes	No
20		6	Yes	No
21		4	Yes	No
22		3	Yes	No
23		6	Yes	No
24		2	Yes	No
25		3	Yes	No

ANSWER KEY

Exercise	Child's Response	Correct Answer	Correct?
26		3	Yes No
27		2	Yes No
28		2	Yes No
29		2	Yes No
30		3	Yes No
31		1	Yes No
32		3	Yes No
33		2	Yes No
34		6	Yes No
35		2	Yes No
36		3	Yes No
37		2	Yes No
38		1	Yes No
39		2	Yes No
40		5	Yes No
41		1	Yes No
42		4	Yes No
43		4	Yes No
44		6	Yes No
45		3	Yes No
46		3	Yes No
47		3	Yes No
48		6	Yes No
49		1	Yes No
50		3	Yes No
51		2	Yes No

Total Correct _____

ANSWER KEY

Exercise	Child's Response	Correct Answer	Correct?	
1		hat	Yes	No
2		banana	Yes	No
3		chair	Yes	No
4		bus	Yes	No
5		bird	Yes	No
6		balloon	Yes	No
7		hand	Yes	No
8		cheese	Yes	No
9		fish	Yes	No
10		kangaroo	Yes	No
11		cup	Yes	No
12		sugar	Yes	No
13		sun	Yes	No
14		kitchen	Yes	No
15		watch	Yes	No
16		grocery store; supermarket	Yes	No
17		comb	Yes	No
18		paper clip; staple	Yes	No
19		backpack; book bag	Yes	No
20		wheel; tire	Yes	No
21		toothbrush	Yes	No
22		lamp	Yes	No
23		piano	Yes	No
24		windows	Yes	No
25		bib	Yes	No
26		helmet	Yes	No
27		thank you	Yes	No
28		match	Yes	No

ANSWER KEY

Exercise	Child's Response	Correct Answer	Correct?
29		chef	Yes No
30		soap	Yes No
31		mailbox	Yes No
32		diamond	Yes No
33		bank	Yes No
34		tree	Yes No
35		curtains; blinds	Yes No
36		fan	Yes No
37		table	Yes No
38		rain; storm	Yes No
39		popcorn	Yes No
40		peanut butter	Yes No
41		pearl	Yes No
42		hammock	Yes No
43		golf	Yes No
44		chess	Yes No
45		Pluto	Yes No
46		signature	Yes No
47		journalist	Yes No
48		script	Yes No
49		mural	Yes No
50		park	Yes No
51		valentines	Yes No
52		a cold	Yes No
53		origami	Yes No
54		tent	Yes No
55		surname	Yes No
56		ticket; fine	Yes No

88 < 87

88 > 87

88 < 87

88 > 87

18
24
21

15
18
21

54

CPSIA information can be obtained at www.ICGtesting.com
Printed in the USA
BVOW07s0742281015

424534BV00016B/62/P

9 780990 848547